IMAGES
of America

AUGUSTA

A *c*. 1870 photograph of Augusta, taken from the Cushnoc Heights. Sprague Mills, the forerunner of the Bates Manufacturing Co., is at left on the riverbank. The white church in the upper right is St. Mary's, with the South Parish Congregational Church to the left. Smith School can also be seen in that same area. Across the river are early buildings of the Augusta Mental Health Institute.

IMAGES
of America

AUGUSTA

Frank H. Sleeper

ARCADIA

First published 1995
Copyright © Frank H. Sleeper, 1995

ISBN 0-7524-0214-5

Published by Arcadia Publishing,
an imprint of the Chalford Publishing Corporation
One Washington Center, Dover, New Hampshire 03820
Printed in Great Britain

Library of Congress Cataloging-in-Publication Data applied for

The Maine State House, as seen
from across the Kennebec River,
one night in the 1950s.

Contents

Introduction

On February 24, 1827, the legislative act making Augusta Maine's state capital was signed. Since that time, politics and government have become an increasingly large part of Augusta life. That life was often centered at the Augusta House, and was highlighted in its earlier stages by the national emergence of James G. Blaine, the 1884 Republican candidate for president who was twice U.S. Secretary of State. Blaine was one of the reasons Maine eventually became a one-party state, one of only two in the nation that voted for Alf Landon in Franklin Delano Roosevelt's 1936 landslide win for re-election as president.

Maine GOP governors often rose up a ladder from local to state legislative posts. Only Democrat Lewis Brann shattered the monopoly in the depths of the Depression. In 1954, the Republican near-monopoly sojourn in Augusta came to an end, partly because of 1952 splits in the GOP, partly because of the stronger Democratic candidates, and partly because of the defection of some of the business interests that had supported the Maine GOP for years.

The last Maine governor to come from Augusta itself was Burton M. Cross. Cross, a florist who had risen through the GOP ranks to become president of the Maine State Senate, was governor from 1953 to 1955. Five generations of the Cross family have lived in the Riverside Drive home where the ninety-two-year-old former governor and his wife Olena reside. Mentally sharp, the former governor made available photographs from his term to the author. As far as is known, this is the first time these photographs from the last Maine governor from Augusta have been published since they appeared during his term as governor. They are included not only because he was the last Maine governor born and raised in the capital city, but also because they give a feel for some of the functions and duties that being governor in Augusta entails.

Cross's term ended with what proved to be a revolution in Maine politics, a revolution which has seen the election of two independent governors in the past twenty years. This revolution continues today, as evidenced in the Maine presidential election scene in 1992, when H. Ross Perot received his highest percentage total of any state in the nation and topped George Bush in a state where Bush had a residence. It remains to be seen whether Maine, like Wisconsin, will become a three party state, or whether it will move back into the two party ranks, as Connecticut apparently has after Lowell Weicker.

One of the essentials in the 1954 political upheaval in Maine was the state's Franco-American population, who held strongly to their traditional Democratic voting. Augusta's Franco-Americans, unlike those in Lewiston and the St. John River Valley, are not a majority. They are, rather, a strong minority. Maurice Violette, in his 1976 book *The Franco-Americans*, postulates that this minority status may have made the Augusta Franco-Americans tougher and more resilient than their sisters and brothers in the majority cities and regions of Maine. I have included in *Augusta* photographs of Franco-American families after they migrated to Augusta between 1890 and 1920. It was a difficult life: many Franco-American families worked in the cotton mills, lived in tenement houses, labored for low wages, and often had to have their children go to work in the mills at very early ages. Later, as Franco-Americans moved upward in the social scale (partly due to the two World Wars), they found other employment, became spread throughout the city and its suburbs, and some, unfortunately, lost the use of the French language and many Franco-American customs. Yet they continued to vote Democratic, partly in protest against their life in Augusta in earlier times.

There was a lighter side to life in Augusta, and I have included images of leisure time activities and sports in the Maine capital. From good simple moments of fun to the teams such as those at Cony High School and the Augusta Millionaires semi-pro baseball team, there are many reminders that life is more than just politics and hard work.

Business has always been important here, and when you turn to business in Augusta, you must turn to Water Street. Water Street was for a long time the business hub of Augusta and the surrounding towns. For much of the period up to 1960, Western Avenue was not as developed by business as it became with the growth of shopping centers. Nestled next to the Kennebec River (as its name implies), Water Street was hilly and eventually became saddled with parking problems. A smaller business area grew up just across the Kennebec River in the eastern part of Augusta, but it never competed with Water Street. There are several photographs in *Augusta* of Water Street in its heyday.

I have also included photographs of the city itself as it grew. For years, Augusta had no zoning. Attempts to set up zoning were defeated year after year as places like Western Avenue grew like Topsy. Finally, a zoning ordinance was passed, but there are many spots in Augusta where the long-time lack of zoning still shows.

In the final chapter I have included the doers and shakers of Augusta—some of them, that is. There are far too many people and places in Augusta's history to cover them all here, and I do not intend this to be a complete history of Augusta. Sources have been discovered while working on this book which need to be developed further. The city has its bicentennial celebration in 1997. There are gaps which must be filled. Materials exist for other pictorial histories of Maine's capital city; hopefully, this will become a reality in the near future.

As has been true of the other four books I've been involved in with the Images of America series, I'd like to dedicate this book to young people, in this case, the young people of Augusta. Looking back a bit at history is never a bad thing to do, especially when it involves your own country. I believe the use of photographs in this series is one of the best methods to bring history to young people, competing successfully with television. For a person interested in the political life of Maine, there is no better place to live than Augusta, a city now much dependent on state government for its economic stability. After all, state workers buy the goods of their lives in Augusta. More power to them.

Frank H. Sleeper

One
Politics and Government

The Maine House of Representatives Hall in 1894. It looks quiet and peaceful but it was not always so. Speeches, not always laudatory, flowed forth. Legislation was passed. There were arguments and dissent. But, in the end, laws were created and the operation of the state maintained. James G. Blaine (see p. 13) was speaker here for a time.

Here's how the State House itself looked in 1894. There have been both additions and subtractions since then.

An 1890s photograph of the home of James G. Blaine, the 1884 Republican presidential candidate. Blaine died January 15, 1893. His home was given to the state by Blaine's daughter, Harriet Blaine Beale, on March 11, 1919. It has been the residence of Maine governors when they are in office since then.

On the arcade at the Maine State House in the 1890s. This image is of a less rushed, less complicated, and generally more peaceful time at the seat of Maine government. Now, the conversations in the State House halls are more animated. Everything is crowded. There are, for example, far more lobbyists, bills, and legislation. Transportation and communication are much more rapid. Legislators now might look at this when they want to relax. It was almost another world at the State House.

The new Augusta House about 1908. For years the deals of Maine legislators were carried out here, in smoke-filled rooms, for good or ill. Located only a couple of blocks from the State House, this hotel was an ideal spot for lobbying, talking, wining, and dining.

Dinner

| Canapes | Oysters |
| COQUELIN | COCKTAIL |

| Consomme a la Madrid | Portage Creme Reine |
| FROMAGE | CROUTONS |

Clam Bouillon
EN TASSE

| BOSTON LETTUCE | CUCUMBER PICKLES | QUEEN OLIVES |

Boiled Salmon, Maitre d Hotel
POTATOES A LA WINDSOR

Butterfish Saute, en Persil
POMMES JULIENNE

| Boiled Leg of Mutton | Boiled Native Fowl |
| CAPERS | SUPREME |

| Virginia Ham Braise | Creamed Chicken |
| WINE SAUCE | EN CASSES |

| Lamb Croquettes | Vanilla Cream Fritters |
| PETIT POIS | AUX FRAISES |

| Roast Ribs of Prime Beef | Roast Leg of Spring Lamb |
| BOILED POTATOES | FRIED PARSNIPS | GREEN PEAS | MASHED POTATOES |

Roast Native Goose, Apple Sauce

| BOILED RICE | STRING BEANS | HUBBARD SQUASH |

✦ Orange Sherbet ✦

| English Walnut Salad | Cucumber and Lettuce Salad, |

Fruit Tapioca Pudding Cream Sauce

✦ Old Fashioned Molasses Apple Pie ✦

Green Apple Pie	Whipped Cream Pie	Hot Mince Pie
Coffee Ice Cream	Assorted Cake
Banana Whips	Raspberry Snow
Layer Raisins	Dates and Figs	Mixed Nuts

| BAHAM SALTINES AND BENT'S WATER CRACKERS | AMERICAN, EDAM AND ROQUEFORT CHEESE |

| Tea | Coffee | Milk |

Augusta House. W. T. Emerson, Mgr.   Sunday, Jan. 31, 1909.

It was good wining and dining. Here is a dinner menu from the Augusta House for Sunday, January 31, 1909. It shows clearly why some legislators might succumb to lobbyists who purchased them meals and drinks.

James G. Blaine, in one of the later pictures taken of him. Blaine was the "Plumed knight of Maine" or the "Continental Liar of Maine," depending upon whom you spoke to. He endured one of the dirtiest presidential campaigns ever in 1884, losing in a close race to Grover Cleveland.

Frederick W. Plaisted was the mayor of Augusta in 1906–08, and again in 1910. Plaisted, a Democrat, was also Maine's governor from 1911 to 1913.

President Theodore Roosevelt comes out of the Blaine House in 1903. Roosevelt, of course, loved Maine. In the area around Island Falls, Katahdin, and the Allagash, Teddy was molded from an asthmatic young fellow into the virile man he personified in later life. Roosevelt kept his Maine guides with him when he purchased a ranch in the Dakota Badlands. They remained his friends as long as he and they lived.

Burton M. Cross receives his gavel as state senate president from his daughter Burtina, *c.* 1950. Looking on are Cross's other daughters, Nancy and Barbara, and his wife Olena. Cross used a gavel made of Maine ironwood which never shattered. Others in Maine, notably long-time Democratic House Speaker John Martin of Eagle Lake, shattered many gavels.

The Cross family getting the results of election night in September 1952. From left to right are: Mrs. Olena Cross, Burtina, Barbara, Governor Burton M. Cross, and Nancy. They are shown at their home on Riverside Drive.

Governor Burton M. Cross is sworn in as the state's chief executive at midnight on Christmas night, December 25, 1952. Cross was sworn in early to fill the unexpired term of Frederick G. Payne, who had been elected U.S. Senator. The ceremony was held at his Riverside Drive home so his mother, Mrs. Harriet M. Cross (in the foreground), could see it. In the back, from left to right, are: Reverend Ackley (the state chaplain), future Maine Supreme Court Chief Justice Robert B. Williamson, Governor Cross, and Mrs. Olena Cross.

At the inaugural luncheon reception in January 1953, Governor Burton M. Cross stands with his wife Olena and two supporters. It was the last time an inaugural luncheon was held: those attending had just become too many.

16

Governor Burton M. Cross delivering his inaugural address to a joint session of the Maine Legislature on January 5, 1953. The occasion is an event of some pomp and circumstance as the governor is led in by a delegation from the legislature. With that address followed later by his budget message, the governor makes his recommendations public and the legislature goes to work—generally ending in some form of compromise by the end of the legislative session, especially if the governor is of a different party from the legislative majority.

Four former Republican governors of Maine line up with Burton M. Cross at his January 1953 inaugural ceremony. From left to right are: William Tudor Gardiner (1929–33), Percival P. Baxter (1921–25), Cross, Sumner Sewall (1941–45), and Lewis O. Barrows (1937–41).

State Representative Albert Cote of Lewiston, one of Maine's largest Democrats, presents Governor Cross with a fox fur because Cote thought Cross was "a foxy man." This took place in the Maine Legislature in either 1953 or 1954. Both Cross and his wife Olena laugh, as does their daughter Burtina.

Governor and Mrs. Burton M. Cross get ready to leave for the first Eisenhower inauguration in Washington early in January 1953. The couple is on the right at the Blaine House.

Governor Cross and party at the inaugural parade for President Eisenhower in Washington on January 20, 1953. It was the last time all the nation's governors appeared in a presidential inaugural parade.

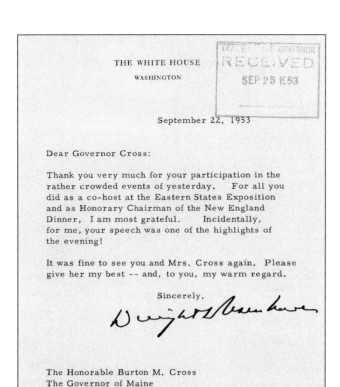

THE WHITE HOUSE
WASHINGTON

OFFICE OF THE GOVERNOR
RECEIVED
SEP 25 1953

September 22, 1953

Dear Governor Cross:

Thank you very much for your participation in the
rather crowded events of yesterday.   For all you
did as a co-host at the Eastern States Exposition
and as Honorary Chairman of the New England
Dinner, I am most grateful.   Incidentally,
for me, your speech was one of the highlights of
the evening!

It was fine to see you and Mrs. Cross again. Please
give her my best -- and, to you, my warm regard.

Sincerely,

Dwight D Eisenhower

The Honorable Burton M. Cross
The Governor of Maine
Augusta, Maine

A letter from President Eisenhower to Governor Burton M. Cross dated September 22, 1953. Cross had supported Senator Robert Taft against Eisenhower in the 1952 GOP presidential primary but, of course, supported Eisenhower for president after the general won the convention nomination.

Former Governor Percival P. Baxter of Maine presents Governor Burton M. Cross with a $950,000 check for the Mackworth Island property that would become the home of the Baxter School for the Deaf. From left to right are: John Willey (Baxter's lawyer), unknown, Roswell Bates (speaker of the Maine House of Representatives), Baxter, Cross, Nathaniel Haskell (president of the Maine State Senate), Norman U. Greenlaw (Maine Commissioner of Institutions), and State Senate Majority Leader Robert N. Haskell.

Governor and Mrs. Burton M. Cross show some of the battleship *Maine*'s silver to officials of the Kittery-Portsmouth Naval Shipyard in 1953. They stand before the official painting of the battleship. The *Maine* was blown up in Havana harbor in 1898, starting the Spanish-American War. The painting left the Blaine House during the Muskie administration, ending up in State Auditor Rodney Scribner's office. It then went to the National Guard in Augusta, according to Cross.

Governor Burton M. Cross, wearing an engineer's uniform, waves goodbye with E. Spencer Miller, president of the Maine Central Railroad, as they get on Engine No. 470 for the final all-day passenger train ride from Portland to Bangor in 1954.

Governor and Mrs. Burton M. Cross attend the Maine chicken festival in Belfast in 1953. The cowboy-type hats were given to the Crosses earlier by the governor of Kentucky. At the same time, Cross had been made an honorary Kentucky colonel. This was a media event, something Cross only did on rare occasions.

Governor Cross is the only Maine governor who has gone down in a submarine. He is shown here at the Kittery-Portsmouth Naval Shipyard in September 1953, on the deck of the submarine *Threadfine*, just before he left aboard that sub.

Governor Burton M. Cross turns his head at the ribbon-cutting ceremony for the high bridge in Augusta in 1953. Next to Cross on the right is former governor, then U.S. Senator, Frederick G. Payne. Cross dedicated the bridge to "John Q. Public, who will pay for it."

Leroy Fogg Hussey, the governor's councillor who ran against Cross in the 1952 Republican primary. The two men were not personally antagonistic, Cross now says, but some of Hussey's relatives didn't like Cross. Both men were from Augusta. Neighbors in that city stopped speaking to each other during the primary. The split carried over into the 1954 gubernatorial election with a strong Republicans for Muskie group being formed, many of them former Hussey supporters.

Governor Edmund S. Muskie, Democrat, shakes hands with outgoing Governor Burton M. Cross, Republican, just after Muskie's inauguration in January 1955. It's doubtful if either man at the time realized just how deep the change was. Says Cross now: "They say that, to succeed in politics, you must be the right man in the right place at the right time. Ed Muskie was all of that."

Two
The Franco-Americans

Democrats and members of Le Club Calumet during the 1954 campaign. From left to right are: (front row) Frank M. Coffin, Edmund S. Muskie, Paul Fullam, James C. Oliver, Rose Hurd (Lewiston), and unknown; (back row) Roland Lessard (Augusta), Noel Lajoie (Augusta), Emilien Laflamme (Lewiston), John Machlin (Waterville), Albert L. Theriault (Lewiston), unknown, Lionel Langlois (Lewiston), and unknown. Le Club Calumet, Augusta's Franco-American club, has close relations with other Franco-American groups in Maine.

At Le Club Calumet's bar in 1952 are, from left to right: Martin Rioux, Roland Lessard, Red LaLiberte, and Lafayette Rancourt. The club was started in 1922 on Water Street in Augusta, moved to Kendall Street in 1935–36, and then to its present location at West River Road (also known as upper Northern Avenue) in 1952. It does all manner of charitable work, and is host to varied meetings. The bartenders here look as if they are ready for a crowd. Most recently, the club was successful in keeping its membership all-male; it does, however, have a large women's auxiliary.

Le Club Calumet first adopted the Pledge of Allegiance as part of its business meeting ritual in 1947. At the first giving of the pledge are, from left to right: Felix Desjardins, Alfred J. Toulouse, Omer Patnaude Sr., Norman Laferriere, Louis Veilleux, Dorilas St. Pierre, Arthur Veilleux, Azarius Paquette, President Paul A. Bouffard, Andrew Tartre, and Sylvio Cote.

Cooking chicken in the 1950s for a Le Club Calumet supper are, from left to right: Chefs Roland Godbout, Conrad Castonguay, and Norman Laferriere.

Some of the first Franco-Americans to settle on the Cushnoc Heights in 1900 pose in front of the St. John Baptist Hall on Kendall Street. They were charter members of the Catholic Order of Foresters. This photograph hangs on the wall at Le Club Calumet. From left to right are: (front row) Edmond Doyon, Elzear Rancourt, Rodolphe Dostie, Napoleon Lajoie, and Ephrem Dostie; (back row) Joseph Castonguay, Napoleon Jolicoeur, Philibert A. "Ti Brom" Poulin, Joseph Parent, and Cyrille Jacquest.

The 50th wedding anniversary of Joseph and Emma Lessard took place at Le Club Calumet in 1952. Shown here are Edmund Bourque (brother-in-law), Emma Lessard, Joseph Lessard, and Midas Lessard.

A Pomerleau Bakery Christmas celebration in the 1930s. Among those present are Mr. and Mrs. Roland Lessard, Armand Demers, Mr. and Mrs. Onasime Soucie, Alfred Beaudoin, Mr. and Mrs. Arthur Lessard (they met while working at Pomerleau's), Eugene Bernier, and Leo Pomerleau (one of the owners).

Roland Demers (left) supervising doughnut production at Pomerleau's Bakery in Augusta, c. 1940s. The bakery was on Franklin Street. Also present were Annette Demers, Germaine Lessard, a Guimond, and two Bretons. As Maurice Violette points out in his 1976 book *The Franco-Americans*, many Franco-Americans started small businesses, especially grocery stores, in the Cushnoc Heights area. Most went out of business eventually; inflexibility in their business practices, Violette maintains, had much to do with these failures. Many, for example, would not do business with banks.

Many Franco-Americans migrated to Augusta between 1890 and 1920 primarily to obtain work in the textile mill in that city. Here are some of the members of one of the spinning rooms at the Edwards Mill, *c.* 1925. From left to right are: (front row) unknown, unknown, Joseph LaChance, ? Rodrique, unknown, and unknown; (middle row) Joseph Quirion (foreman), unknown, unknown, Juliette Grondin, unknown, unknown, and Miss Greenleaf; (back row) unknown, unknown, unknown, Celina Cyr, Rose Morrisette, Mrs. Turcotte, John Quirion, and Cleophis LaChance. Typical wages were $3.50 a week for a 54-hour week.

Such wages were not conducive to high living. The Quirion family stands by its tenement house, *c.* 1890s. The Augusta Fuel Co. was later located here.

The loom room of the Edwards Mill before the turn of the century. Those identified here are: (front row, left) Mssr. Breton; (middle row, left) Mssr. Mathieu; (middle row, right) Mssr. Cote; (back row, fourth from left) Joseph Lessard; (back row, second from right) Stanislas LaMontagne.

Officers of Local 493, Textile Workers Union of America, in the Edwards Mill, *c.* 1939. From left to right are: (front row) George Poulin, President Roland Lessard, and Napoleon Veilleux; (back row) Noel Lajoie, Leo Paul Nadeau, and Florian Dumont. The union provided the Franco-Americans of Augusta with a means to obtain better wages and was a rallying point for them, much like Le Club Calumet.

Celebrating fifty years at the Edwards Mill are, from left to right: (front row) Ellen Sirois, Philamon Dumont, unknown, and Joseph Lessard.

A c. 1930s photograph of Pete Quirion, an Edwards Mill fixer

Some of the Lessard family with Matt Koral, the general manager of the Edwards Mill, in the 1940s. Included here are: Raoul, Valmont, and Leo Lessard; Matt Koral; and Valere and Roland Lessard.

Tenements and clothes lines in the Franco-American section of Augusta in 1938.

Le Club Calumet, the bastion of Franco-American strength in Augusta, at its Kendall Street location in 1938.

B. Cloutier was a Franco-American business in Augusta in 1938.

Ovide Pomerleau, meats and groceries. This 1938 photograph shows an example of the most common type of Franco-American business in Augusta during the years immediately after their migration.

The Wilfred Patenaude store in 1938. Patenaude's was one of the longest-lived businesses in the Cushnoc Heights area (also known as Sand Hill).

The Perrault Paint Store in 1938.

B.J. Cote Insurance in 1938.

These Franco-American veterans of World War I are shown on the steps of the St. Augustine Church in 1918, after the war's end. They were honored at a banquet here. Church officials, relatives, and friends are also on the steps. World War I, of course, built relationships with

France for this nation's Franco-Americans—at least for those who fought in France. It also provided the Franco-American troops with broader horizons.

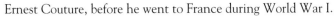
Ernest Couture, before he went to France during World War I.

Ernest Couture in France, where he was killed during
World War I. Franco-Americans from Augusta had
an excellent record in the "War to End All Wars."

Amide Couture (right) is shown here during World War I.

It was 1939, two years before the United States entered World War II. These were members of Company F, Second Battalion, 103rd Infantry, Maine National Guard from Augusta. A good number of Franco-American names are included. Membership in the guard was one way to make a little extra money—and to be patriotic at the same time. From left to right are: (front row) G.S. Dennett, C.C. Simard, A.G. Bechard, C.V. Haskell, A. Pullen, F.T. Hammond, M.G. Small, and F.R. Turcotte; (middle row) A.G. Tardiff, C.J. Matthieu, A. Harvey, J.W. Lovell, C.J. Cormier, R.A. Rancourt, A.G. Cote, R.T. Waugh, and H.L. Hammond; (back row) G.G. Thibault, L.M. Rollins, L.F. Johnson, E.P. Mandosa, R.F. Bradbury, L.E. Davis, R.L. Rancourt, G.E. Demos, and H.L. Norton.

Edmund Violette and his wife, Therese St. Amant Violette, were in St. Hyacinthe, New Brunswick, Canada, when this photograph was taken. They were the parents of thirteen children, including Maurice, and they migrated to Augusta to obtain mill jobs there and improve their economic lot.

Part of the Violette family at their 14 Bond Street home in 1922. Addie is at the rear; in the front are Jeannette, Maurice (aged four months), and Rita.

Four years later, the Violette family is shown once again at its Bond Street home. From left to right are: (front row) Maurice and Rita; (second row) Jeannette, Claude, Aurele, Edgard, and Addie; (third row) Rudolphe, Nellie, Edmund, Therese, and Anthony. Roland Veilleux, a neighbor, is on the left. Maurice Violette recalls sleighing down the State Street hill on barrel staves with a wooden seat, and being stopped from doing so at night by St. Mary's Church people.

For one or two years, the Violette family lived over a meat market in Augusta. However, as Maurice recalls it, the cockroaches there proved to be too much and the family moved to 3 Crosby Street. Shown there in 1933 are, from left to right: (front row) Lorraine Grondin (a niece), Jeannette, and eleven-year-old Maurice; (back row) Therese, Addie, Edmund, Claude, Louis Lemieux (Addie's husband), and Edgard (a nurse at the Togus Veterans' Facility).

Jeannette and Maurice Violette pose by the family car at their Crosby Street home in 1935. The family's economic lot was improving a bit in spite of the Depression.

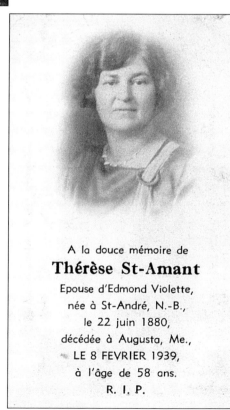

A la douce mémoire de
Thérèse St-Amant
Epouse d'Edmond Violette,
née à St-André, N.-B.,
le 22 juin 1880,
décédée à Augusta, Me.,
LE 8 FEVRIER 1939,
à l'âge de 58 ans.
R. I. P.

Therese Violette died on February 8, 1939.

Maurice Violette with Florence Cyr Dulac in the 1940 Chizzle Wizzle production of *Show Boat* at Cony High School. Although he had an excellent voice, Maurice didn't have too much time for extracurricular activities. During his senior year at Cony, he also had to work a night shift at the cotton mill to help the family's finances. It was a typical example of what happened in many Franco-American families in Augusta; as difficult as it was, however, there were points in time when children began working much earlier in their lives.

Maurice Violette wears hand-me-down clothes for a 1941 wedding in Augusta. This was standard in large Franco-American families. World War II gave Maurice a way out from the probability of working in the mill. He enlisted in the navy in 1942, shortly after Pearl Harbor, and spent twenty-years in that service. Many young Franco-Americans from Augusta followed similar routes.

Maurice enlisted on January 13, 1942. He was made a buck sergeant in boot camp when it was discovered he could run a mimeograph machine, but was only paid at the apprentice seaman's level for four months. He became a petty officer, third class.

Maurice Violette in Recife, Brazil, late in 1943. He eventually visited forty-five different countries during his career in the navy, gaining a broad knowledge of languages and customs.

Maurice visiting the home of his wife, Esther Margaret Birt, on Page Street, Augusta, on December 31, 1942. With the couple is her father, James W. Birt. The couple was married for forty-seven years.

Maurice Violette's brother Edgard was a sergeant when he was photographed in Auckland, New Zealand, in March 1944. Edgard was drafted in 1939.

People on the steps of the St. Augustine Church in the Cushnoc Heights during a funeral in the early 1920s. The church and the strong religious feelings of its parishioners was one of the strengths of Augusta's Franco-American population.

This 1950s photograph, taken in the Cushnoc Heights, is another example of the strength of religion among Augusta's Franco-Americans. From left to right are: Reverend Gerard Patenaude, Sister Florence Patenaude, and Reverend Laurent Patenaude. They were sister and brothers.

Another strength that Augusta's Franco-Americans could buttress themselves upon was the St. Augustine School. These are the 1922 graduates of that school, the first year it was accredited. From left to right are: (front row) Annie Pepin, Irene Lambert, Regina Pelletier, and Emilio Lambert; (back row) Remi Labbe, Laurent Laflamme, Henri Lahaye, and Emile Poulin.

An earlier graduating class of the St. Augustine School, before the school was officially accredited. The diploma of Joseph Fortier is in front. This is a *c.* 1910s photograph.

50

These are the 1935 graduates of the St. Augustine School. From left to right are: (front row) Normand Daniel, Blanche Quirion, Diana Labonte, Roland Thibault, Bernadette Poulin, Allan Rodrique, Violette Roy, Joseph Poulin, Sebastienne Ouellette, and Emery D'Auteuil; (middle row) Murielle Poulin, Louise Labbe, Alice Lemieux, Anita Cloutier, Lionel Dumont, Lucille Toulouse, Rita Bilodeau, Doris Labbe, and Rosanne Castonguay; (back row) Geraldine Poulin, Lucienne Fortier, Rita Violette, Murielle Chaput, Yvette Roy, and Gerard Michaud. Every name is Franco-American.

Here are the 1936 St. Augustine School graduates. From left to right are: (front row) Lucille Roy, Juliette Machildon, Imelda Giroux, Anna Arbour, Anita Gilbert, Constance Gilbert, Alcea Maheux, Lucille Dulac, and Fernande Godbout; (middle row) Rita Melancon, Rita Plante, Madeleine St. Hilaire, Roland Michaud, Lucien Levesque, Maurice Violette, Renaud Doyon, Armand Beaulieu, Marianne Roy, and Marie Rose Dubreuil; (back row) Andre Levesque, Robert Beaudoin, Armand Beaulieu, Emile Quirion, Roland Arbour, Roland Blanchette, Leo Albert, and Richard Martin. Once again, all the names are Franco-American.

Perhaps the greatest strength of the Franco-Americans, in Augusta and all over Maine, was and is the strength of the family. A mother reaches out to a tot with a clothesline, fence, road, and hill in the background. Nothing could be more symbolic of that family strength.

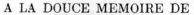

A memorial to Marie Trahan (the wife of Joseph Quirion), who died in Augusta on April 24, 1929, at the age of fifty-five.

A family picture of Aime, Lionel, Arthur, and Gilda Veilleux, *c.* 1930.

Robert Veilleux, *c.* 1930. Robert died in July 1936, when he fell in the Patenaude barn near his home.

More family pictures. This is the Quirion family in the 1880s. Joseph is in the front left, while Charles is in the back center.

Joseph Quirion and his wife, Marie Trahan Quirion, c. 1910s. Marie Anna Quirion, mother of Ted Veilleux, is in the center of the three children.

54

The Lessard family in the 1920s. From left to right are: Leo, Etionette, Valare, Roland, and Arthur.

The Lessards in 1939. From left to right are: (front row) Raoul, Joseph (the father), Etionette, Leo, Emma (the mother), and John; (back row) Roland, Arthur, Nelson, and Valare.

Joseph and Emma Lessard with their children, Jeannette and Raoul, at home in the 1930s.

Henri Grenier and his wife, Sylvia Gagne Grenier, in the 1910s.

Three family men. From left to right are: Raoul Couture, unknown, and Larry LaFlamme.

Perhaps this is a Texas sheriff-type, like Wyatt Earp. No, it is Joseph Couture of Augusta in the 1910s.

The St. Augustine School in 1938. This elementary school is still in operation, and the education it provides is one of the basic strengths of Augusta's Franco-Americans.

The 1935 Le Club Calumet baseball team. From left to right are: (front row) Sylvio (Turk) Gilbert, Leo Lemay, Richard Poulin (bat boy), Romeo Cote, and Doria Breton; (middle row) Paul Poisson, L. Gilbert, C. Watts, Robert Marks, and Dominic Lacasse; (back row) Albert Aube and Alphonse Poulin.

Three
Sports and Leisure

Life was not always serious in Augusta, in spite of some of the hardships that had to be endured. Here is a group of women and men horsing around in the 1920s or '30s. The men lie down in front while the women are in the back row. Included here are Leo Brunelle, Amide Couture , Mrs. Romeo Jolicoeur, two Castonguay girls, and one Lausier girl.

Leo Brunelle and a Cloutier girl kick up their heels in the 1920s.

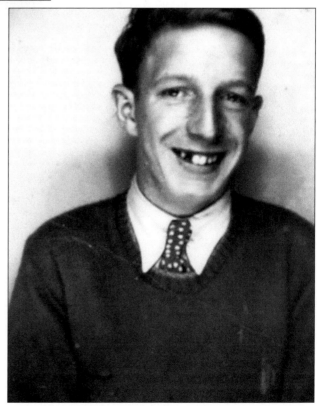

Aime Veilleux, in a photograph taken at a Gardiner carnival in 1940. Carnivals move all over Maine even today.

Two gentlemen hamming it up on snowshoes in 1925. It is believed they are Larry Laflamme and Jerome Lausier. Snowshoeing was very popular all over Maine in the 1910s and '20s, but later fell off in popularity. In recent years, it has made somewhat of a comeback. It was part of the simpler entertainment of those earlier days.

And here are nine gentlemen really hamming it up in front of a house in the 1920s. Included are Oscar Pepin, Jerome Lausier, Larry Laflamme, and Henri Veilleux.

Jerome Lausier is the man in front with the skis, while Ruth Lausier is the girl in the background. The woman with Jerome remains unidentified.

This child is having a great time in the snow in the 1920s. After a while, when it got cold, it was time to retreat inside for some hot cocoa.

Here are some celebraters in the bouncing 1920s. Included are Dominic Cloutier, Oscar Pepin, Alexina Couture, Odile Castonguay, and Ruth Lausier.

Matilda Couture is in the lap of a man from New Hampshire in this 1920s photograph.

Three couples kiss it up in Augusta in the 1920s. Madeleine and Armand Lambert are involved, as is Cleo Couture in the middle. These were simple pleasures in a less complicated time.

A mock wedding played out by the children of some of Augusta's more eminent families about 1900. From left to right are: (front row) Ada Plummer, Mary Stinson, Beth Golder, Marian Woodman, Marguerite Lowell (Locke), Florence Gannett, Cony Weston, Nathan Weston, unknown, and Lee Hersey; (back row) Genie Norton, Harold Hichborn, Philip Hayden, Blanche Webster, unknown, and unknown.

The Augusta Trolley League baseball champions of 1906.

A band at Island Park in the 1930s. The resort was especially popular during the 1930s and '40s. Big Bands sometimes played here on Cobbosseecontee Lake. Among the most popular local big bands were those of Lloyd Rafnell and Al Corey.

Togus Pond in Augusta was a popular place for cottages and year-round homes. This is Camp Norman Kearney, a cottage, in 1938.

These circus posters were up in 1938. Russell's Circus was coming to town on July 3. Circuses have always been immensely popular.

Rebecca was playing at the Colonial Theater in 1938.

A bird's-eye view of Lake Cobbosseecontee about 1910, with a cottage in the foreground. Augusta people have cottages now on both Cobbossee and Togus Ponds; both are within easy driving distance of Water Street and the business center of Augusta.

Rifle practice during a state muster near what is now the Augusta Airport on August 16, 1894. The use of guns has always been extensive in Maine for hunting, and this is especially true in northern Maine. The pro-gun sentiment is also strong in central Maine and the rural sections of southern Maine. Dr. Alonzo Garcelon, an Augusta dentist, was president of the National Rifle Association for a year. Dr. Garcelon is dead. But there is still plenty of pro-gun sentiment left in the state.

One of five sturgeon captured in the Kennebec River below Augusta, possibly in the 1870s or '80s. Sturgeon can weigh up to 300 pounds. There was an interest then to put the fish in a mill pond above where this one was photographed. Pollution ended the appearance of sturgeon in the Kennebec for years. With the river's semi-cleanup, there have been some reports of their reappearance.

The undefeated Cony High School state champion football team of 1932. Coach Bill Macomber is in the center with, from top right to bottom right, counter-clockwise: Stan Washuk, Dick Braley (later principal of Erskine Academy), Dominic Lacasse, Don Grimshaw, Dick Sawyer, Normie Merrill (the best football player in the state, though only a sophomore), Bob Coakley, ? Mclaughlin, Carl Barnes, Dudley Tyson, Lionel Foyt, Arthur Payson, and Burleigh Roderick.

The 1938 Cony High football team with its members' weights. From left to right are: (front row, the line) George Burney, 175 pounds; Paul Cyr, 165; Ted Dempsey, 175; Curley Speare, 165; Ken Pierce, 145; George Perkins, 170; and Floyd Tillson, 170; (back row, the backs) Ralph Smith, 150; Joe Murphy, 165; Bud Wing, 150; and Frank Haines, 168. Football players were lighter then. George Mendall was the coach.

The 1953 Cony High football team. From left to right are: (front row) N. Woodward, J.Whitney, O. McCullum, W. Ross, S. Tardif, D. Katon, P. Gilbert, J. Davis, G. Tarrio, and K. Dolley; (second row) C. McArthur, D. Watson, R. Kaler, M. Riley, G. Quirion, W. Barden, K. Bunker, W.Endicott, W. Brown, R. Deschaine, and J. Gallant; (third row) R. Rand, C. Paddle, R. Burdzell, R. Gagne, R. Hastings, G. Black, R. Smith, R. Davis, D. Schmidt, M. Burns, and R. St. Pierre; (back row) C. Jones, K. Pruett, Coach Fran Parker, C. Arbour, and J. Kersey.

The 1959 Cony High football team went 6–3. One of its victories was over Portland High. From left to right are: (front row) Bill Howe, Larry Coughlin, Dick Small, Ray Roy, John Smith, Pat MacFarland (co-captain), Bob Gosselin (co-captain), Dave Caron, Bill Browne, Doug Allen, Lou Boucher, and Bob Browne; (second row) George Demos, Mike McNally, Tom Barden, Gerry Theriault, Ken Pruett, John Hastings, Carlton Barter, George Hill, Pat Perrino, and Dennis Finnemore; (third row) Dan Sherwood, Charlie McDonald, Bob Greene, Hector Doyon, Tom Eaton, Bob Degon, Ken Robie, and Jack Shrader (manager); (back row) Lionel Fortin, Vince Dostie, S. Legg, Bob Vachon, Rick Parent, Don Whitney, Head Coach Bob Whytok, and Assistant Coach Larry Dyer.

Andy Lano of the Augusta Millionaires looks out after scoring at Capitol Park, Augusta, in a 1948 game, the first year of the Millionaires' existence. Norman Merill, one of Cony High School's greatest athletes, is the umpire. The look is to see just how many bases the hitter will take.

Andy Lano scoring in a 1948 Augusta Millionaires night game, at Capitol Park. The catcher is probably from the Eastern Paper Corporation team of Brewer. The Millionaires, through an arrangement with the Boston Red Sox, had future Red Sox like Ted Lepcio, Harry Agganis, and Haywood Sullivan as players. The players lived in Winthrop in the same boarding house used by the pre-World War II Winthrop Mills team, put together while Alan Goldfine was operating those mills.

The 1951 Augusta Millionaires team. From left to right are: (front row) Dick Bergquist, Jim Greene, John Watson, Bob Webber, Dick Knoblauch, Bob Schults, Ed Yaeger, and Val Doyon; (back row) Sylvio (Turk) Gilbert, Haywood Sullivan (later a catcher and executive vice president and part owner of the Boston Red Sox), George Risley, Bert Helgerson, Ben Houser (manager), Larry Keller, Dave Quinn, Tony Blose, and Jackie ?.

Horsing around at Lily Bay, Moosehead Lake, on July 4, 1938. Pictured here are Edward Martin (front), his wife Denise, Napoleon Cloutier, and Ted Veilleux.

Four

Business

The Market Square Grocery Store and Chandler and Boardman on busy Water Street, *c*. 1890s.

Water Street, Augusta's business district, after the 1865 fire.

Water Street with horses in the foreground, *c.* 1890s.

Water Street, the hub of Augusta business activity, in 1938.

Gofkauf's automotive store stood out in the Augusta business district in 1938.

The Nicolson & Ryan jewelry store, a fixture on Water Street in 1938. For many years it was presided over by former Maine State Senator Bennett Katz.

The R.B. Herrick Co., located on Water Street, sold gifts, housewares, luggage, and toys in 1938.

Depot News, the Water Street spot where you bought your papers and magazines in 1938. It's still selling papers and magazines, though the nearby railroad depot is no longer.

The Depositors Trust Company on Water Street in 1938.

Another bank on Water Street, the First National Granite Bank, in 1938.

A bank photograph from the 1940s. From left to right are: Richard E. Goodwin, Guy C. Longfellow, Charles (Pete) West, and Mrs. Mary Witt.

Kirschner's, which later grew into a much larger company and moved its meat processing facilities off Water Street, and the Royal Hotel in 1938.

The Hussey Hardware Company, the store of 50,000 items in the sub-business district across the Kennebec River on Bangor Street in 1938. The store was operated by the Hussey family from 1921 to 1995.

The A & P (Great Atlantic & Pacific Tea Company) store on Bangor Street in 1938. The A & P was started by George Hartford, an Augusta native.

The Pineland Diner and Wayside Inn on the east side of the Kennebec River in 1938.

Fowler's Market in Augusta in 1938. Note the Moxie sign. Moxie was first put together in Lisbon Falls, Maine. It still survives.

Remember the signs for products that used to be on the sides of barns and other structures? This barn in Augusta was advertising Old Scotch Ginger Ale in 1938.

The Augusta Lumber Co. in 1938.

The Augusta Tallow Co. on Mount Vernon Avenue in 1938. That company, of course, no longer exists.

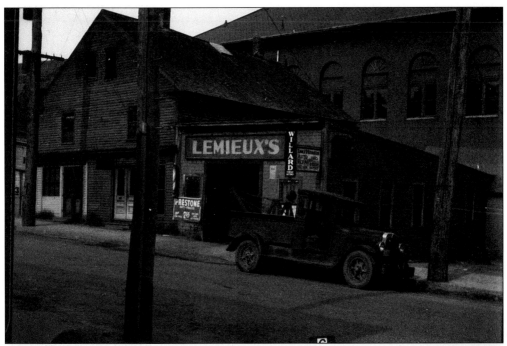

All businesses in 1938 were not in the best buildings. This is Lemieux's, which sold, among many other things, Prestone and Willard batteries.

Do we still have cobblers around operating under that title? In 1938, Marceau & Son in Augusta proudly announced what it did, not calling itself a "shoe repair location."

Note the 1938 prices at Mrs. McGrath's Candies, Ice Cream and Home Made Lunches in Augusta. A hot dog was 10¢, as was a hamburger. Coffee was only 5¢.

They are Exxon gas stations now, but in 1938 they bore the Colonial Esso label.

The *Maine Farmer* Publishing Office in 1879, opposite Haymarket Square in Augusta. This Greek Revival-style building remarkably survived the fire of 1865. It is presumed that it was demolished about 1885 to make way for the U.S. Post Office Building.

Menu

DRESSED CELERY   QUEEN OLIVES

Grape Fruit
FRAPPE

Bluepoints
COCKTAIL

Mock Turtle a la Anglaise
QUENELLES

Filet of Red Snapper, Mousseline
POMMES NOISETTE

Mignons of Beef Bordelaise

POTATOES JULIENNE   STRING BEANS

Asparagus Tips on Toast
CREAM SAUCE

Augusta Board of Trade Punch

Roast Squab au Cresson

SWEET POTATOES   HUBBARD SQUASH

Lobster Salad
HOT ROLLS

Harlequin Ice Cream

Angel Cake   Macaroons

Crackers   Cheese

Cigars   Cigarettes   Coffee

The menu for the annual banquet of the Augusta Board of Trade, November 12, 1908. This shows that Augusta business had its own organizations years ago.

A white horse in front of a millinery store on Water Street in the 1870s.

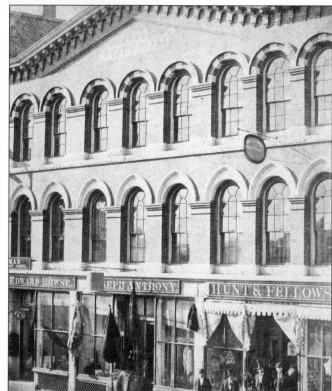

Hunt's Block on Water Street, *c.* 1866. Some of the businesses in this view include Edward Rowse, Joseph Anthony, and Hunt & Fellows.

The Kennebec
Cotton Mills,
c. 1890s. This was
once the old
Edwards Mill.

The machine shop at
the dam in Augusta,
looking east across the
Kennebec River,
c. 1890s. The dam is
still controversial.
Should it be removed
to aid in the restoration
of fish in the river?

Augusta has had many manufacturing operations besides its textile mills. This is the Eaton Shoe Company, *c.* 1920.

The Vickery-Hill Publishing Co, *c.* 1910. It produced such magazines as *American Woman*, *Needlecraft*, *Good Stories*, *Happy Hours*, *The Farm World*, and *Hearth & Home*.

The steamer *Augusta*, *c*. 1870s.

The Maine Central Railroad station in Augusta, *c*. 1890s. It no longer exists.

Transportation didn't always go smoothly in Augusta. These trains collided at Brown's landing by Riverside on May 18, 1883. But, generally of course, things moved along well. There was once passenger rail service to Maine's capital city, but no longer. There were trolleys and street railways to other central Maine communities. A case might be made that transportation facilities in Augusta were better years ago than they are now.

Five
The City

The covered bridge at Augusta over the Kennebec River, *c.* 1900.

The Fuller Observatory was 162 feet high, with 12 stories. It was 544 feet above the level of the Kennebec River, c. 1890s.

A postcard of the Augusta Post Office published by *Comfort Magazine* of Augusta, the first magazine in this country to have a circulation of one million. It cost 10¢ a year, *c*. 1900.

The Granite Block fire destroyed Granite Hall on December 30, 1890. It was 22 below zero during the blaze. After the fire, the Opera House replaced Granite Hall.

Soldiers of the Spanish-
American War, c. 1898, in
Market Square.

The Cony House, c. 1890s.

St. Mary's Catholic Church, *c.* 1900s.

Governor Hill's residence on State Street, later the Oblate Retreat House.

The Administration Building of the Veterans Administration Facility, Togus, c. 1940s. This is basically a veterans' hospital.

THE THEATRE AND HOSPITAL, VETERANS ADMINISTRATION FACILITY, TOGUS, MAINE   1679

The theater and hospital of the Veterans Administration Facility, Togus, c. 1940s.

A view looking east of the Maine Insane Asylum (now the Augusta Mental Health Institute), c. 1870s. This is one of the oldest hospitals for the mentally ill in the country. Its second superintendent was Isaac Ray, one of this country's most famous psychiatrists, who worked closely with Dorothea Dix, a native of Hampden, Maine, to bring the mentally ill out of jails.

Another eastern view of the Maine Insane Asylum, c. 1870s. It's interesting to think about how Dr. Ray and Miss Dix would view the status of the mentally ill in much of this country now. In trying to place them back into the community, have we sentenced them to be homeless or put them back into jails?

A northeast view of the Maine Insane Asylum, c. 1870s. Now the Augusta Mental Health Institute, this facility has maintained a generally fine reputation in its more than 150 years of existence.

The Augusta State Hospital in the 1890s. The hospital expanded greatly in the twentieth century as it reached a peak population of over 1,700.

Some idea of just how much the Augusta State Hospital (AMHI) expanded can be obtained from this 1950s aerial photograph. Under the superintendency of Dr. Francis H. Sleeper, the institution reached its population peak in the late 1940s and early 1950s, and then fell as drugs to alleviate mental illness were discovered. But today, who or what insures that these suffering people will take their drugs once in the community?

The Soldiers Monument in Augusta. It was erected in November 1881 and dedicated on September 21, 1882. Made of granite, it was 50 feet high and cost a total of about $10,000.

The Kennebec Dam looking east across the river, c. 1890s.

The George A. Cony residence on the Cushnoc Heights, c. 1890s. Cony was a prominent Augusta businessman, philanthropist, and civic-minded citizen.

Augusta City Hall, with ladies walking across the bridge in front of it, *c.* 1908.

Gone but not forgotten. A dead moose at Camp Keys, Augusta, on May 7, 1917.

The first stage of the construction of the U.S. Post Office in Augusta, *c*. 1900.

The Augusta waterfront, *c*. 1900, with the post office on the left and, above it, the steeple of the Methodist church. In the right hand corner of the picture the dome of the Kennebec County Jail can be seen.

The No. 5 Mail Car of the Augusta, Winthrop, & Gardiner Street Railway, *c.* 1910s or 1920s.

The Giant Oxien Co., Augusta, *c.* 1900. Giant Oxien was a cure-all product heavily advertised in *Comfort Magazine*, which was also owned by William H. Gannett.

The Arsenal, c. 1900. It was located close to the east side of the Kennebec River, below the Augusta Mental Health Institute.

Cony High School, Augusta, c. 1910.

Lakehurst Farm, Lake Cobbosseecontee, *c.* 1900.

The Augusta City Hospital, *c.* 1906.

Under the Augusta bridge during the 1936 flood.

The water in back of a Water Street hotel during the 1936 flood.

Six

Doers and Shakers

Elzear Rancourt, an Augusta policeman, *c.* 1920s.

Joseph Quirion, the chef at the Togus Veterans Administration Facility, *c.* 1920s.

A *c.* 1921 photograph of Roland Lessard, taken when he was six or seven years old. Lessard would become a long-time employee of the Edwards Mill and eventually be the president of the Textile Workers Union of America local there.

Joseph H. Manley, a Republican leader from Augusta and a close friend of James G. Blaine.

Edwin C. Burleigh was the governor of Maine from 1888 to January 1893, and succeeded James G. Blaine in Congress. Born in Linneus in Aroostook County, he moved his permanent residence to Augusta in the 1880s. William Pattangall says in his *Maine Hall of Fame* that Burleigh controlled the *Kennebec Journal* in Augusta "just like Blaine did." Burleigh eventually became a huge timberland owner.

Huntington Hartford, a member of the family which founded the A & P grocery chain, visits the Hartford House in Augusta in 1915.

Farnsworth Marshall, the principal of Cony High School, in 1910.

Granville P. Cochrane was on the city council during the Civil War and was the Augusta city clerk in 1868. He is shown here in 1870.

Maine Supreme Court Justice William R. Pattangall, c. 1930s. Pattangall in his *Meddybemps Letters* and *Maine Hall of Fame* may have been the state's leading political satirist of all time. First a Republican, then a Democrat, then a Republican, Pattangall was named to the Maine Supreme Court on July 2, 1926, was named chief justice on February 7, 1930, and resigned from that post on July 16, 1935. He lived in Augusta from 1915 until his death there on October 21, 1942. He was also the first president of the Depositors Trust Company, the forerunner of the Key Bank of Maine.

Robert B. Williamson was chief justice of the Maine Supreme Court from October 4, 1956, to August 21, 1970. Williamson was in a law film with Pattangall for several years after Pattangall resigned as chief justice. A gentle gentleman, Williamson was born in Augusta on August 23, 1899, and died there December 28, 1976. He was a fourth generation lawyer but always maintained, after working for the *Harvard Crimson* and the *Kennebec Journal* one summer, that he might have liked to be a journalist. Active in civic affairs, he was a past president of the Congregational Christian Conference of Maine and was chairman of the Conference of Chief Justices (national) in 1967.

An 1880 photograph of Llewelyn Lithgow, founder of Augusta's public library, the Lithgow Library.

Daniel Cromett Clark, a native of South Paris, was a reporter and writer on the *Kennebec Journal* in 1903. This photograph was taken in 1889.

Daniel Robinson (1777–1866) was the editor of the *Maine Farmer's Almanac*, published in Augusta.

Mrs. Hannah Dillingham, preceptress of the Cony Female Academy, on her ninety-second birthday, on June 16, 1880. Her husband was Pitt Dillingham.

Reverend George R. Palmer, pastor of the Green Street Methodist Church in Augusta from 1886 to 1889, c. 1885. Palmer was also a lieutenant colonel in the 19th Maine Regiment.

"General" Jacob Arnold (1797–1882) spoke at a protest meeting in the city government in 1849. This photograph was taken in the 1860s.

Henry F. Hill, who had two dogs, Merry and Christmas, which he dressed in coats when it was cold. He was an Augusta character who was fond of telling Wild West stories in which, he said, he had taken part. Hill died at the age of ninety in the 1950s.

The bust of Joshua Chamberlain in the State House rotunda. Chamberlain was an amazing man: a former Maine governor, he was also a Civil War hero of Gettysburg, a general, and the president of Bowdoin College.

Ah, youth. Willis R. Partridge at the age of four in the 1890s.

118

Dr. Francis H. Sleeper, a relatively poor boy from Houlton who rose to become assistant commissioner of mental health for Massachusetts and returned to Maine in 1946 as the superintendent of the Augusta State Hospital (now AMHI). He was superintendent until 1963 when he retired because of Parkinson's disease. After his retirement, he worked on planning for the future of mental health care in Maine. The president of the Augusta Rotary Club in 1953, he received an honorary doctor of science degree from Bowdoin College as well as the highest health awards granted in this state.

William H. Deering, the former Maine state finance officer and later long-time treasurer of the Augusta State Hospital, c. 1940s.

Dr. Grace R. Foster was a psychologist at the Augusta State Hospital.

A c. 1900s photograph of Guy P. Gannett with a big catch. Gannett was the founder and president of the Guy Gannett Publishing Company, which owned three Maine newspapers, television and radio stations in several states, and other publications. He is shown here in his teens.

Guy P. Gannett as the commodore of the Augusta Yacht Club in the 1910s. Gannett lived in Augusta the first forty-five years of his life, moving to Cape Elizabeth, a Portland suburb, in 1927. At various points he was on the Augusta City Council, was both a state representative and a state senator, and was a member of the Republican National Committee. He purchased the two Portland morning newspapers in 1921 and combined them into the *Portland Press Herald*.

Guy P. Gannett, a lifelong aviation enthusiast (he was a founder of the Civil Air Patrol during World War II), with Charles Lindbergh in the late 1920s.

William H. Gannett, the founder of *Comfort Magazine* and the father of Guy P. Gannett, on his ninetieth birthday on February 10, 1944. He is shown here cutting his birthday cake in the city room of the *Kennebec Journal*, while *Kennebec Journal* employees look on.

William H. Gannett (right) and his son, Guy P. Gannett, at the controls of a plane at the Augusta Airport in the 1930s or '40s.

William H. Gannett and his son
at the wedding of one of William
Gannett's granddaughters,
c. 1940s.

Governor Henry S. Cleaves and
the Maine State House, *c*. 1895.

Lory Bacon (1783–1860) of Augusta. We know little about him, other then that he was born in Charlton, Massachusetts, on October 31, 1783, married Hannah Hamlen of Augusta on November 15, 1812, died in Augusta on August 4, 1860, and was a Mason.

Mrs. Abbie Allen, the aunt of Orville Dewey Baker, in 1871.

Jane Howard (1782–1869), *c.* 1860s. Jane was possibly related to the Howard family which had the first trading post at Cushnoc (Augusta).

Louis Bouffard, an Augusta milkman, *c.* 1900s.

Roland Roy, an Augusta shoe factory worker, squirrel hunting in a quarry at the Cushnoc Heights, *c.* 1922.

Aime Veilleux and Omer Beaudoin, one of his friends during World War II.

Still having a good time at Moosehead Lake on July 4, 1938, are Edward Martin, Antonia Dumont, and Ted Veilleux.

The Britt House was the first dwelling in Augusta.

Acknowledgments

The road to obtaining the photographs for this book started with Augusta City Manager Terry St. Peter, who gave many leads and told me of the 1938 city assessment photographs. Terry directed me to Anthony Douin of the Kennebec Historical Society, who gave all kinds of help. I had met Maurice Violette, a co-member of the committee to organize the 150th anniversary celebration of the Augusta Mental Health Institute, and remembered Maurice was an authority on the history of Augusta's Franco-Americans. Maurice had, indeed, written The Book on that subject. He supplied photographs himself and took me to Gloria Morrisette, Edward and Aime Veilleux, Roland Lessard, and Lawrence Laflamme, all of whom graciously supplied photographs. Maurice was a great help.

Anthony Douin and I spent several afternoons at the University of Maine at Augusta library going over and selecting the Historical Society pictures which were used. Douin directed me to Earle Shettleworth, director of the Maine Historic Preservation Commission, who went way out of his way to see that I received almost one hundred photographs, postcards, and stereoscopic slides from the Commission. Douin also directed me to Mike Burns, owner of Burnsie's in Augusta, who provided me with Cony High School football team pictures and who directed me to Andy Lano in Falmouth for Augusta Millionaire photographs. In turn, Lano directed me to Dave Quinn of Portland for a Millionaire team photograph.

Possibly the greatest coup eventually resulted when Douin directed me to Alan (Barney) Roach, a long-time photographer for the *Kennebec Journal*, now retired, who had me contact Clarence McKay in Gardiner. Clarence told me that former Maine Governor Burton M. Cross had several scrapbooks of photographs from his term as governor from 1953 to 1955.

The former governor, the last Maine governor to come from Augusta, didn't seek any publicity but was very cooperative in selecting photographs for use here. At age ninety-two, his mind is as sharp as ever and he was certainly a big help.

For last minute help with very necessary photographs, I have to thank Christopher Beam, director of the Muskie Archives at Bates College, Mrs. Lois Griffiths of the archives, and Richard Hussey of East Winthrop. John Gannett directed me to and Deborah Rumery helped me select the Gannett pictures.

I sincerely hope I've left no one out. Much more work remains to be done on the pictorial history of Augusta. Finally, I'd like to thank Kirsty Sutton and all the crew at Arcadia for the great help along the way. This is my fifth effort for them. I hope there will be many more. Eventually, I may be able to meet a deadline without being in a rush.

All thanks to everyone.

Frank H. Sleeper